A HISTORY OF BRITAIN IN...

12

Fashion Items

PAUL ROCKETT

W
FRANKLIN WATTS
LONDON • SYDNEY

Franklin Watts
Published in paperback in Great Britain in
2018 by The Watts Publishing Group

Editor: Sarah Peutrill
Design and illustration: Mark Ruffle
www.rufflebrothers.com

Dewey number: 746.9'2'0941
ISBN: 978 1 4451 3615 8
Library ebook ISBN: 978 1 4451 3616 5

Printed in China

Franklin Watts
An imprint of
Hachette Children's Group
Part of The Watts Publishing Group
Carmelite House
50 Victoria Embankment
London EC4Y 0DZ

An Hachette UK Company
www.hachette.co.uk

www.franklinwatts.co.uk

Picture credits:
Archive Photos/Getty Images: 26t; Silviya Arsova/
Dreamstime: 28b; Bombaert/Dreamstime: 23t;
© The British Library Board: 14; Classic Image/
Alamy: 4bl; Condé Nast Archive/Corbis: 26b;
Devonshire Collection/CC Wikimedia: 21c; C
M Dixon/AAA Collection/Alamy: 6; geni/CC
Wikimedia: 10b; Geo/Alamy: 10c; Gryffindor/CC
Wikimedia: 20tl; Claudia Hake/Shutterstock: 7cr;
David Hanlon/Dreamstime: 29br; Hatfield House/
BAL: 16b; IT Photo/istockphoto: 27t; Jastrow/
CC Wikimedia: 13br; Jonbod/CC Wikimedia: 7t
Matthias Kabel/CC Wikimedia: 9cr; Keasebury
Gordon Collection/Alamy: 22br; Petr Kratochvil/
Public Domain Picture/CC Wikimedia: 4cr; Leeds
Museums and Art Galleries/BAL: 18t; LOC/CC
Wikimedia: 4br; Pavel Losevsky/Dreamstime:
front cover bc, 27b; John McClellan/Mary Evans
PL: 25t; Met Police Authority/Mary Evans PL:
24t; Monkey Business/Dreamstime: front cover
bl, 29tl; NPG/BAL: front cover cl, 5t,16tr; NTNU
Vitenskapsmuseet/CC Wikimedia: 11br; A Dagli
Orti/Art Archive/Corbis: 10cr; Parema/istockphoto:
28t; Reptonix/CC Wikimedia: 9bc; Reuters/Corbis:
5c; The Royal Collection. © Her Majesty Queen
Elizabeth II 2014/BAL: 17b; Mark Ruffle: 19t;
Saliko/CC Wikimedia: 9l; Sotheby's/CC Wikimedia:
19b; Linda Spashett/CC Wikimedia: front cover
t, 8; Terence's Comedies/CC Wikimedia: 13l;
Tichborne House, Hants/BAL: 19c; Evgeny Tomeev/
Shutterstock: 25b; Herr Uberman/CC Wikimedia:
20br; ultramarinphoto/istockphoto: 29bl; Nadezda
Verbenko/Shutterstock: 29tr; CC Wikimedia: front
cover cr, cb & br. 5b, 12cl, 12cr, 12b, 15t, 16tc, 17t,
18b, 20tr, 20bl, 21bl, 21br, 22t, 22c, 23bl, 23br,
24b; Colin Young/Dreamstime: 11t; Jiri Zuzánek/
Dreamstime: 15br.

*Every attempt has been made to clear
copyright. Should there be any inadvertent
omission please apply to the publisher for
rectification.*

CONTENTS

DRESSING UP BRITAIN

Today, Britain is a leading force in fashion. It's home to some of the best designers and most photographed models in the world, helping us decide what to wear.

British clothing has varied throughout the country's history. The clothes have ranged from the cheap and most practical garment available, to the most extraordinary and impractical.

National costumes

Many countries have a national costume. This acts as a symbol of their identity, and may come from a period in history when the outfit was commonly worn.

England doesn't have a national costume. However, many people associate England with the outfits of the Queen's Guards (above) or pearly kings and queens.

The national dress of Scotland is the kilt. It was originally worn by Scottish Highlanders in the late 16th century, with fabric draped over the shoulder.

The Welsh national costume was worn by women in the Welsh countryside, around the 18th century. It features a long shawl and a tall hat.

British icons of fashion

Fashion icons are people we look to for inspiration on the clothes we wear.

Royal fashion icons

Royalty have long played an important role in leading fashion trends, buying and commissioning the top designs and the finest materials. Key fashionable Royals include Tudor monarchs (see pages 16–17), King Charles II (see page 19) and Kate, the Duchess of Cambridge.

King Charles II, painted in the 1660s. Charles II sought out the finest tailors, buying suits from Paris and London.

Industry insiders

Fashion became a big global industry in the 20th century and Britain has produced some of its top designers, such as Vivienne Westwood, Alexander McQueen and Stella McCartney.

Fashion designer Stella McCartney (right) with British-born Anna Wintour (left), editor of Vogue, *one of the most influential fashion magazines.*

Celebrity style gurus

Celebrities have also led the way in fashion. These include poets and adventurers like the 2nd Earl of Essex (1565–1601), Georgian socialites (see pages 20–21), actors, musicians and footballers, like David Beckham.

The 2nd Earl of Essex cut a dashing figure at the Tudor court (see pages 16–17).

The following fashion items...

The following pages highlight 12 items that show the changing fashions and fortunes of Britain, helping to reveal Britain's history.

The choice in the clothes we wear today owes a debt to the fashions of the past, and these fashions may well return in the future. The clothes included here may help you pick out your next outfit!

CLOTHING CLUES

We know very little about what clothes in Britain looked like during its early history. Most of the materials that were worn have rotted over such a long period of time. However, many tools and accessories have survived providing some clues as to how people dressed.

Bones and stones

We know that early Britons wore animal fur and skins from the clothing tools that have been discovered. These tools include flints used for cutting and needles made from animal bones. These discoveries date back to Neolithic times (6000 BCE– 2500 BCE).

Stone weights have been found that date back to the Bronze Age (2500 BCE–800 BCE). These stones were used on a loom to make cloth. Textiles made of vegetable fibres and wool were woven on a loom by hand.

This is a reconstruction of an Iron Age loom. It shows how stone weights held down the threads to keep them tight while threads were woven across them.

Torcs

1

The majority of clothing artefacts that have survived are metal objects. During the Iron Age (800 BCE–43 CE), metalworkers became more skilled in making weapons and tools, as well as jewellery. Necklaces and brooches from this period often have complex designs, and are made up from lots of small pieces of precious metals.

Many torcs have been uncovered from this period. These are neck bracelets that marked the wearer out as being a person of high importance.

This is the Great Torc from Snettisham in Norfolk. It's made from 64 threads of gold mixed with silver.

Clothing facts

Some fragments of clothing have survived. A leather shoe from the Bronze Age was found in Somerset. Archaeologists in Denmark have discovered woollen jumpers from the Bronze Age. These survived as they were buried in deep mud that preserved them.

In Iron Age Britain, many different coloured dyes were used to colour clothes. These were made from plants and berries.

The leaves of the woad plant were used to produce a dark blue dye.

In 50 BCE, the Greek historian Diodorus Siculus wrote down a description of what the British wore. It included:
"shirts which have been dyed and embroidered in varied colours, and breeches [trousers that come down to the knee]. They wear striped coats, fastened by a buckle on the shoulder."'

TUNICS AND TOGAS

When the Romans settled in Britain, the tunic became the standard dress for all, worn by slaves and nobles, adults and children. The cold weather in Britain, however, meant that extra layers of clothes were also needed in order to keep warm.

Cold Britannia

When it was cold, several tunics were worn over each other. Men also wore trousers and a cloak. Women wore a shawl, called a *palla*. The palla was draped around their shoulders or worn over their head like a hood.

Many people kept slaves who helped them dress. Some households had up to 500 slaves. Slaves were captured in battle and sold at slave markets, both in Britain and abroad.

The wealthy wore clothes made of fine wool, linen and silk. The slaves' clothes were made of cheap wool. In cold weather slaves wore a rough woollen cloak over their tunic.

Men and women wore their tunics at different lengths, as shown on this Roman tombstone from Yorkshire. The father and son wear them to their knees and the mother to her ankles.

Togas

2

The toga was an outfit that could only be worn by Roman citizens, a status held by many Britons during Roman rule.

The toga was a semicircular piece of cloth wrapped around the body and draped over the left shoulder. It was off-white in colour, with variations depending on your status. Senators wore togas with a purple band. Roman emperors had togas that were coloured with the most expensive dye – 'imperial purple' – made from sea snails.

Roman boys and girls dressed the same as their parents. This statue of a Roman boy shows him wearing a toga.

Roman soldiers also wore tunics, but on top wore protective armour, such as chainmail or body plates. The type of helmet and clothing worn showed your rank.

A copy of a centurion's helmet. The crest on top helped their men follow them into battle.

Those who worked outdoors, such as farmers and soldiers, wore long woollen stockings and leather shoes. A letter found at Hadrian's Wall tells us that soldiers wore socks. The letter is from a soldier's mum and in it she mentions sending him socks from home.

The Romans washed their clothes in either urine or a chemical called sulphur.

THE COARSE AND THE REFINED

In Anglo-Saxon England, the rich and poor all wore simple long-sleeved tunics belted at the waist. This style of dress lasted for many centuries.

Tunics and brooches

Poor families wore tunics made from coarse wool, spun and woven by the women and girls of the family. If you were wealthy, your tunic was made from fine wool and linen.

The wealthy could afford to wear tunics dyed in expensive shades of red or blue, whereas poor people's clothes were often left undyed.

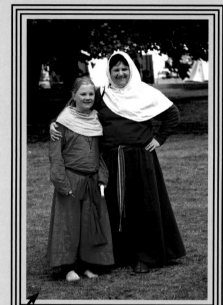

Re-enactors dressed in Anglo-Saxon tunics. Children wore smaller versions of their parents' clothes.

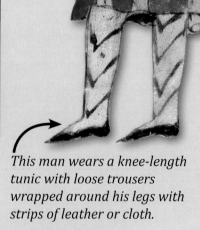

This man wears a knee-length tunic with loose trousers wrapped around his legs with strips of leather or cloth.

In cold weather people wore thick woollen cloaks fixed in place with brooches. The brooches were usually made of bronze, but were more highly crafted the richer you were. The wealthy had brooches decorated with gold, silver and precious stones.

This 7th century brooch is decorated with gold and glass. It was found on a farm in Norfolk.

3

Sutton Hoo helmet

The tunic was a practical outfit for farming and daily life. However, all Anglo-Saxon men, even farmers, were expected to fight for their king. Going into battle, they wore chainmail over their tunics, with a helmet and shield for protection.

The most impressive Anglo-Saxon helmet was found buried in Sutton Hoo in Suffolk and dates from the 7th century.

The helmet was made for a king or a great warrior. It's covered in images of birds, dragons and boars believed to protect the wearer.

The helmet shows the great skill Anglo-Saxon craftsmen had in design and metalwork. It was built to impress and protect, but also for comfort. The face mask was lined with leather and has holes under the nose plate for the wearer to breathe through.

In this replica of the helmet we can see a bird's body forming the warrior's nose, the tail his moustache and the wings his eyebrows.

Clothing facts

Anglo-Saxons were skilled embroiderers. The wealthy had the ends of their tunics embroidered with patterns from nature, such as a looping ivy branch.

When the Vikings arrived in Britain in the 9th century, they wore domed helmets, without horns. It's thought that they looked much like this 10th century helmet found in Norway.

EMBROIDERED HISTORY

In 1066, William the Conqueror came to England from Normandy, France. The Bayeux Tapestry tells the story of his army's victory over the Anglo-Saxons. This huge embroidered cloth, completed over ten years after the Norman invasion, gives us an insight into what people wore at that time.

French fashions

In the Bayeux Tapestry, the Anglo-Saxons and the Norman men can be told apart by differences in hairstyle and dress.

The Normans are clean-shaven, some have moustaches, and their hair is shaved around the back of their necks.

The Anglo-Saxons are shown with long hair and some have beards.

The Anglo-Saxons are shown wearing tunics, whereas the Normans are shown wearing *culottes*, baggy French breeches that end at the knee.

Only three women appear in the tapestry. One woman is shown fleeing a house set on fire by Norman soldiers. Although the woman is Anglo-Saxon, her dress shows a French fashion for long drooping sleeves.

The bliaut gown

4

The Normans brought French fashion into the English court. The French gown, known as a *bliaut*, was popular with the wealthy. It gave the wearer an elegant shape, with a tight waist and long sleeves that drooped down from the elbow.

The sleeves were often so long that they were sometimes knotted to stop them dragging on the ground.

The length of the sleeve was a sign of your wealth. It reflected the amount of money you could afford to spend on the material.

A woman wearing a bliaut, from a 12th century English manuscript.

The Norman conquests made silk more widely available in Britain. It was imported from the Norman territories in the south of Europe, such as Sicily.

Many Flemish weavers came to settle in England during this time. They were famous for making the finest woollen fabrics. Their expertise helped to improve the quality and design of fabrics made in England.

Craftsmen, such as weavers and tailors began to form guilds. These were groups that protected the interests of your profession.

It became fashionable for women to wear their hair long, often with large plaits hanging either side of the head, as shown in the statue of William's wife, Matilda. To make their hair appear longer, women attached fake hair, ribbons and silk tubes.

CRIMINAL CLOTHING

During medieval times, merchants became richer as a result of increased trade. They displayed their new wealth by wearing clothes like those of noblemen and women. The nobles saw this as a threat to their position, and so laws were passed banning people from wearing certain clothes and materials.

What not to wear

In 1363, King Edward III passed a law that listed what women from different classes were not allowed to wear:

- *Wives and daughters of servants must not to wear veils above twelve pence in value.*

- *The wife or daughter of a labourer must not to wear clothes beyond a certain price.*

- *Only women of the royal family can wear cloth of gold and purple silk.*

The poor were not concerned with copying the changing fashions of the nobles. Their clothes were practical and made from coarse wool, changing little during this time.

This illustration, from the early 14th century, shows a peasant woman wearing a kirtle, a close-fitting outer-garment. The woman is also holding a drop spindle, a tool that spun wool into yarn. She sold the yarn or used it to make her own clothes, such as her kirtle.

5

The poulaine shoe

Throughout the 14th century, long pointy-toed shoes, known as poulaine shoes, were fashionable for men.

The poulaine shoe had a toe that had been known to measure up to 60 cm in length. Its long toe was often stuffed with moss and whalebone to keep it stiff.

Having long shoes was a sign of high status. A clothing law passed in 1335 allowed only wealthy men to wear shoes with a toe longer than two inches. The law stated that:

"no knight under the estate of a lord, esquire or gentleman, nor any other person, shall wear any shoes or boots having spikes or points which exceed the length of two inches, under the forfeiture of forty pence."

This 15th century French painting shows the poulaine shoe being worn by servants.

Clothing facts

There were lots of ferrets and beavers living wild in medieval Britain. Their fur was used to line the inside of clothes for warmth. Fur was also used for decoration around the neck and cuffs. Sheepskin, badger and cat were worn by the lower classes. Finer furs, such as ferret, fox and squirrel, were worn by the wealthy.

People wore a variety of headwear, ranging from hooded capes and felt cones to straw hats. The wimple, covering the whole of a woman's head, was popular and was adapted as a habit for nuns.

Ferret fur was popular with the wealthy.

RUFF STUFF

The Tudor monarchs enjoyed wearing elaborate outfits made with the finest materials and decorated with expensive jewels.

Tudor fashionistas

King Henry VIII wore doublets (tight-fitting jackets) that were padded to make his upper body appear broad and muscular. This look became popular during his reign and continued after his death in 1547.

Henry VIII padded the codpieces he wore over his groin, sometimes keeping jewels inside them.

Henry's sixth wife, Catherine Parr, wearing a Spanish farthingale.

Henry's first wife, Catherine of Aragon, was from Spain. She made the Spanish farthingale popular. This was a cone-shaped frame worn inside a petticoat. It pushed out the skirt creating a triangular shape.

This painting, A Fete at Bermondsey (1569), shows both the wealthy and poor. On the left, the wealthy women and girls wear Spanish farthingales; on the right, the poor are dressed in kirtles (see page 14).

Tudor monarchs spent fortunes on clothing to stay ahead of fashion and inspire awe in their subjects.

Queen Elizabeth I wore elaborate and expensive ruffs – a piece of neckwear that became popular during her reign (1558–1603).

Worn by both men and women, the ruff was made from starched linen or lace. It was often worn in layers with pleated folds.

Some ruffs were known to stick out up to 20 cm from the wearer's neck.

This portrait of Elizabeth I is from 1588. She is celebrating her defeat of the Spanish, and wears a ruff of the finest lace.

Clothing facts

In 1571, a law was passed that all lower-class people should wear woollen caps on Sundays and public holidays. This law was created to support the wool trade in England.

In the late 16th century, men in the Scottish Highlands wore kilts. These began as a large tartan cloak draped over most of the body and one shoulder (see page 4).

Queen Mary I wore high-heeled shoes to make her appear taller. High-heeled shoes became popular with rich women and also men, leading to the phrase 'well-heeled', referring to men of wealth.

Slashing clothes and pulling out the cloth from the undergarment, became popular.

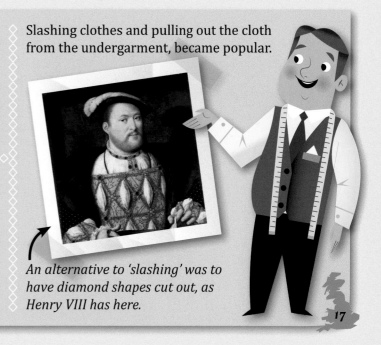

An alternative to 'slashing' was to have diamond shapes cut out, as Henry VIII has here.

PLAIN PURITANS

After the English Civil War (1642–1651) England was without a monarch for 10 years. Out went King Charles I and his lavish court to be replaced by Oliver Cromwell and his strict government. Cromwell frowned upon expensive and elaborate decorations. He preferred a plain and simple form of lifestyle and dress for everyone.

Plain and simple

As a Puritan, Oliver Cromwell believed that people should lead godly lives.

He believed that people should dress in plain and practical clothes. Dark clothes with little or no colours were favoured, with plain white linen collars. Many Puritans also wore tall, wide, black hats. This hat became known as the capotain.

Oliver Cromwell (1599–1658)

Capotain

7

Capotains were worn by men and women but were most common amongst older poor women.

The capotain is also known as a Pilgrim's hat. It became a symbol of the early settlers in America. In 1620, a group of English Puritans known as 'Pilgrim Fathers' set sail to North America. They set up one of the first English colonies, and named it New England.

Portrait of a middle-class lady wearing a capotain

In 1660, King Charles II returned to England from France to reclaim the throne. He was known for his love of fashionable clothes and was influenced by the styles of the French court.

Charles II. and his Queen, from Heath's Chronicle, 1662.

This illustration shows Charles II and his wife Catherine. As Charles' reign continued, his clothes became less fancy, featuring fewer ribbons and bows.

In the 17th century, stays (an early name for a corset) were worn by women as bodices on the outside and top half of a dress. They made the waist thinner and gave the body a V-shape.

For the wealthy, lace became the must-have material, used on cuffs, collars and handkerchiefs. It was extremely costly and it took a long time to make even the smallest piece. In 1662, Parliament banned the import of Flemish lace, in the hope that people would wear lesser quality English lace.

This painting, from 1671, shows a local landowner distributing bread to the poor. To the right, the poor are mainly dressed in plain overcoats with many capotain hats sticking out from the crowd.

Here, King Charles I (1600–1649) wears a wide lace collar that became a fashionable replacement for the ruff.

WIG OUT

Wealthy people in Georgian Britain saw a lot of changes in fashion. Many looked to Europe and to the young icons at the royal court for ideas on what to wear.

Extremes of elegance

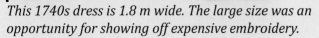

On formal occasions, many wealthy women were forced to walk into a room sideways through the door. This was because they wore really wide skirts. They were created with large hoops underneath their petticoats.

By the end of the 18th century, a more simple 'Empire line' style of dress became popular. This was a high-waisted dress that flowed downwards in a straight line.

This 1740s dress is 1.8 m wide. The large size was an opportunity for showing off expensive embroidery.

In the 1770s, a group of wealthy young men, known as Macaronis, dressed in extreme versions of fashions discovered from touring Europe.

This 1773 caricature of a Macaroni highlights their fashion for giant wigs and striped stockings.

A longer lasting influence on men's fashion came later from the Prince Regent's friend, Beau Brummell. His look, known as that of a 'dandy', became the standard outfit for men by the 1820s.

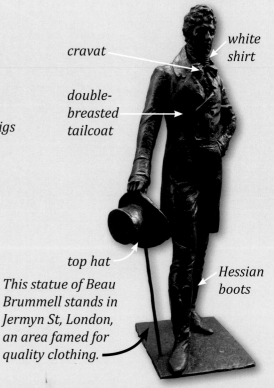

cravat

white shirt

double-breasted tailcoat

top hat

Hessian boots

This statue of Beau Brummell stands in Jermyn St, London, an area famed for quality clothing.

8

Wig

Towards the end of the 18th century, wigs and hairpieces reached extreme heights. Fashion icon, Georgiana, Duchess of Devonshire, favoured tall wigs topped with long feathers, including ostrich feathers, which could be one metre high.

Often the wigs were so tall that women had to crouch on the floor to prevent the wigs from being crushed and set alight as they brushed past candle-lit chandeliers.

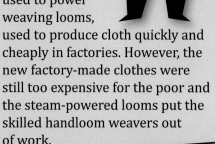

Georgiana, Duchess of Devonshire (1757–1806)

Stuffed birds were often popular decorations on wigs. This caricature, drawn in 1775, shows fashionable French visitors to London with birds flying to nest in their wigs.

Clothing facts

The Industrial Revolution began in the 18th century. It was a time when steam engines began to power large machines. In 1785 steam was being used to power weaving looms, used to produce cloth quickly and cheaply in factories. However, the new factory-made clothes were still too expensive for the poor and the steam-powered looms put the skilled handloom weavers out of work.

Before steam, giant handlooms were used, like these from the 1740s.

The fashions of the rich were at the expense of the poor. Embroiderers often went blind due to working long hours in candlelight, and the new factories left many skilled workers penniless. Many poor people were forced to live in workhouses. Families were split up; men and women lived separately and wore plain uniforms. Women worked doing laundry or sewing. The conditions were often dreadful.

BUSTLES AND BOWLERS

The population of Britain more than doubled during Victorian times. More factories were built to meet the demand in food and clothing. Children worked in cotton mills, where conditions were harsh and noisy and accidents were common.

Shifting shapes

The very rich could still afford to have clothes handmade for them by skilled tailors and dressmakers.

Wealthy women had outfits made that changed the look of their body shape. The crinoline and the bustle changed the proportions of the lower body. Corsets were worn pulled tight to give the wearer a tiny waist.

This woman is receiving help to put on her dress over a crinoline, a hooped frame that was fashionable during the 1850s and 60s.

This lady is wearing a bustle. The bustle is a frame worn under the skirt, padding the behind to make it look larger. It became popular from the 1870s.

The poor had neither new factory clothes or the latest fashions from dressmakers. They wore plain woollen or second-hand clothes. Poor children often had adult clothes cut to fit them.

These street urchins are wearing clothes not dissimilar to adults.

Bowler hat

Men's fashion centred around the three-piece suit of waistcoat, trousers and jacket. The material worn varied depending on your wealth – woollen cloth for the poor and fine cottons with silk waistcoats for the wealthy. Working-class men wore cloth caps, while upper-class gentlemen wore a top hat.

The bowler hat was designed in 1849.

Clothing facts

This advert shows a woman wearing bloomers for cycling. Cycling became popular towards the end of the 19th century. It gave women more freedom and led to the demand for practical garments, like bloomers. Originally called 'Turkish dress', bloomers were promoted as a comfortable choice in women's clothing.

The hard bowler hat was designed originally for the working-class outfit of a gamekeeper. The hat was to protect his head from low-hanging branches while on horseback. It became popular with the middle and upper classes and is nowadays associated with businessmen in the City of London.

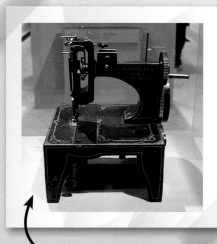

This is the prototype of the sewing machine invented by American Isaac Singer.

During the Crimean War (1853–56) the 7th Earl of Cardigan wore a knitted military style jacket. After the war the style caught on in Britain, and became known as the cardigan.

The first successfully mass-produced sewing machine became available in the 1850s. It meant that clothes could be made and mended at home quickly and easily.

During the Second World War (1939–45), clothing factories and materials were used to make parachutes and uniforms for soldiers. Clothing was rationed and new clothes were scarce.

Clothing coupons

Everyone was given a Clothing Book with coupons that allowed people to buy clothes. The more fabric and labour that was needed to produce a garment, the more coupons were needed to buy it.

Clothing rations in 1945:
an overcoat: 18 coupons
a man's suit: 26–29 coupons (according to lining)
men's shoes: 9 coupons
women's shoes: 7 coupons
woollen dress: 11 coupons.

These children are being sent from a big city to go and live in the countryside. Known as 'evacuees', they were asked to take a clean change of clothes and strong walking shoes with them.

A poster from the 'Make Do and Mend' campaign.

Children's clothes needed fewer coupons in recognition of the fact that children outgrow their clothes quickly.

A 'Make Do and Mend' campaign was launched to encourage people to patch up and recycle old clothes that could still be worn.

Trousers for women

Because clothes were rationed, many women began to wear their husbands' clothes, including their trousers. With men away serving in the armed forces, more women were employed in factories and on farms where trousers were practical work-wear.

It became increasingly acceptable for women to wear trousers which were specifically made for them. By 1944 sales of women's trousers were five times higher than they had been in the previous year.

This woman wears the uniform trousers of the Women's Land Army. This was an organisation formed during the First and Second World Wars, where women took over the farm work left by the men who went to war.

Clothing facts

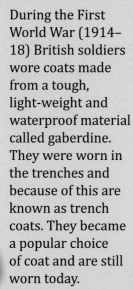

Nylon stockings first went on sale in 1940. They were extremely popular, but the war made them hard to come by. Women often painted fake seams up the back of their legs to give the impression that they were wearing a pair of stockings.

During the First World War (1914–18) British soldiers wore coats made from a tough, light-weight and waterproof material called gaberdine. They were worn in the trenches and because of this are known as trench coats. They became a popular choice of coat and are still worn today.

Post-1945 TRIBES

After the hardships of the war years people wanted to experience a sense of luxury. By the late 1950s families were better off and teenagers had spare cash to spend on leisure and clothes. Youth culture led the way in fashion; influenced by American films, popular music and an urge to be rebellious.

Gangs and grunge

Different looks came to be associated with movements and gangs.

The 1950s was the era of the Teddy boys. Their style was like that of the dandy, wearing suits copied from the early 1900s.

In the 1960s there were clashes between two main gangs, the mods and the rockers. The mods wore suits and large overcoats; the rockers wore leather jackets and had greased back hair.

In the 1960s there was also the hippy movement, a peaceful group with long hair, flowery clothes and flared trousers.

In the late 1970s punk appeared. This was a reaction to the everyday and was built around loud and aggressive music. There was a DIY approach to clothing, featuring safety pins, bin liners, spikey hair and tartan.

Punks with fashion designer Vivienne Westwood (right)

Music continued to inspire the fashions of the 1980s, with theatrical outfits from bands known as the New Romantics. In the 1990s, fans of grunge music wore second-hand clothes, inspired by American bands like Nirvana.

The mini

The 1960s in Britain are often called the 'Swinging Sixties'. Pop music and fashion were made by and for young people.

British bands, such as The Beatles, were hugely successful around the world and London became a focus for fashion. Designer Mary Quant and models, such as Twiggy, made the mini skirt popular.

The mini skirt, or mini, became a symbol of the decade and its celebration of youth.

Revealing women's legs was seen as radical. However mini skirts were usually worn over a pair of tights. Tights replaced the shorter leg stocking and became widely available in the 1960s, allowing the skirt's hemline to rise above the knee.

Clothing facts

In the 1990s, supermodels became famous. These were highly paid and glamorous models who posed for magazine covers and walked the catwalk at fashion shows. British models Naomi Campbell and Kate Moss became supermodels.

Catwalk shows became big events and helped establish the supermodels' fame.

Denim jeans started out as work-wear in mid-19th century America. They became increasingly popular in Britain from the 1960s and have been adapted by different movements. They were worn flared by hippies and were worn ripped by punks and grunge fans.

21st century
FASHION REVIVALS

The 21st century has seen a revival of many clothing styles from the 20th century. Formal, old-fashioned clothes, described as vintage, have become popular, while casual wear associated with sports and youth are worn by people of all ages.

Old and sporty

Some people buy their clothes second-hand, wearing 1950s summer dresses and tweed jackets. These styles have also inspired new designs.

Summer dresses inspired by 1950s fashion, displayed in a shop window

Sportswear on sale in a department store

Brand names, such as Nike and Abercrombie & Fitch, have become important status symbols, particularly in sportswear. Designers known for working in high-end fashion, such as British designer Stella McCartney, have created tracksuits and gym gear for sportsmen and women.

The hoodie

The hooded top, or hoodie, was an item of sportswear originally popular in American hip-hop culture. During the 2000s, it became associated with gang culture. It was a uniform that allowed members to hide their identity under the hood, while being up to no good.

A brief fashion trend saw body suits designed for babies – onesies – being made and worn by grown ups.

However, the hoodie has since become an item of clothing worn by everyone, from toddlers to old-age pensioners.

A recent craze for loom bands has children all around Britain weaving rubber bands into jewellery. This has seen the loom come a long way from the weighted stones of Bronze Age homesteads to a small and portable item popular in the playground.

The comfortable feel and casual look of the hoodie has made it popular.

Further information

Books

Britannia: Great Stories from British History by Geraldine McCaughrean (Orion, 2014)

The Story of Britain by Mick Manning and Brita Granström (Franklin Watts, 2014)

Timeline History: Clothes by Liz Miles (Heinemann Library, 2011)

Tracking Down series by Moira Butterfield (Franklin Watts, 2013)

Websites

What clothes did people wear during the First World War? Explore this BBC Schools website to find out:
www.bbc.co.uk/schools/0/ww1/25268180

Information and images guiding you through British fashion of the wealthy from 1050 to the 1960s:
www.historic-uk.com/CultureUK/FashionthroughtheAges/

Children's British History Encyclopedia featuring a timeline with detailed information from each era and information on finding and interpreting historical evidence:
history.parkfieldict.co.uk/

Website for the Fashion Museum in Bath, allowing you to explore the collection and enlarge images of different outfits from Britain's past:
www.fashionmuseum.co.uk

Explore fashion on the Victoria and Albert Museum's website:
www.vam.ac.uk/collections/fashion

Glossary

artefact
an object that has historical interest, such as the remains of past human life

bustle
a frame with padding worn under a skirt to make the behind appear larger

casual
relaxed and informal; clothes for everyday wear

caricature
a drawing that's made to make the subject look silly

crinoline
a hoop or hoops fitted into a petticoat that is worn under a long skirt to make it stand out

embroidery
decorations sewn onto cloth

evacuee
a person moved away from a place of danger to somewhere safe

farthingale
a cone-shaped frame worn under the skirt

icon
a figure held up to great acclaim

import
to bring in goods to sell from abroad

Industrial Revolution
a period when society began using machines and factories for producing goods, approximately between 1750–1850

influence
to have an effect on something, such as changing a style within fashion

inspire
to be a point of reference for something, such as a creation or a change in fashion

kirtle
an outer-garment worn as an overall to keep clothes underneath clean, closely fitted to the body

loom
a tool used for making fabric by weaving together wool or thread

merchant
a person who buys and sells goods, especially with other people in foreign countries

Neolithic
early period of history, also known as the last stage of the Stone Age, when stone tools, pottery and farming developed

nylon
a strong, lightweight, elastic material made from a chemical process

petticoat
a loose hanging skirt worn as an undergarment beneath a dress or skirt

pilgrim
a person who travels to a foreign place, often connected with religion

pleat
a fold in a piece of cloth held in place by stitching

Puritan
a member of a Protestant Christian faith that believes in strict religious discipline

reign
period of rule by a king or queen

socialite
a person who is well-known in society and attends lots of fashionable events

status symbol
an activity or object that suggests a person's position in life

textiles
material woven or knitted together, such as cloth

trend
a popular appearance of an activity or object

tunic
loose garment made from two rectangles of cloth sewn together, originally sleeveless

Index